LU & CLANCY'S
SECRET CODES

ASMLTIPZL
SEBEHSUZE

QIKURU
UCHRYP

ADOWLDSOE
NYUILICVR

WOONPETEU
HDGAPDHPP

written by **Adrienne Mason**

illustrated by **Pat Cupples**

Kids Can Press

Kids Can Press acknowledges the financial support of
the Ontario Arts Council, the Canada Council for the
Arts and the Department of Cultural Heritage.

Published in Canada by   Published in the U.S. by
Kids Can Press Ltd.   Kids Can Press Ltd.
29 Birch Avenue   85 River Rock Drive, Suite 202
Toronto, ON M4V 1E2   Buffalo, NY 14207

Edited by Valerie Wyatt
Designed by Julia Naimska
Printed in Hong Kong by Wing King Tong
Company Limited

CM PA 99 0 9 8 7 6 5 4 3 2 1

Canadian Cataloguing in Publication Data

Mason, Adrienne
 Lu & Clancy's secret codes

(Lu & Clancy)
ISBN 1-55074-553-0

1. Cryptography – Juvenile literature. 2. Ciphers –
Juvenile literature. I. Cupples, Patricia. II. Title. III.
Title: Lu and Clancy's secret codes. IV. Series.

Z103.3.M37 1999   j652.8   C99-930312-0

For Angus — AM
For Maimie — PC

Kids Can Press is a Nelvana company

Contents

Two Dogs Inc.

Psst!

"Psst, Clancy."

Clancy stopped dead in his tracks. "That's weird — I thought I heard that bush call my name."

"You did," whispered the bush. "It's me — Lu."

Clancy peered into the bush and sure enough, there was his best friend.

How it works

1. Lu wrote the message in reverse code. To decode it, just reverse the letters in each word.

EIHPOS = SOPHIE

Can you decode the message Lu sent to Clancy? (Answer on page 40.)

2. When you're writing reverse code, you can make the code harder to break by adding commas, periods or other punctuation anywhere you like.

EIHPOS SI, NO RUO LIART TEEM. NI EERT ESUOH TA. RUOF!

What are Lu and Clancy up to? I'm going to find out.

"I'm avoiding my pesky little sister," Lu explained. She looked around nervously, then whipped out a pink balloon and handed it to Clancy. Before Clancy could say a word, Lu was gone.

Clancy knew just what to do — he and Lu had been studying secret codes for weeks. He took the Two Dogs Inc. pin off his collar and popped the balloon. Inside was this piece of paper.

EIHPOS SI NO RUO LIART.
TEEM NI EERT ESUOH TA RUOF.

3. Want a code that's even tougher? Reverse the words as well as the letters.

RUOF TA ESUOH EERT NI TEEM LIART RUO NO SI EIHPOS.

4. Now try breaking the words up in different ways.

RUOFT AESU OH EERTNI TE EMLIART RUON OSIE IHPOS.

?GODAD NA GORFAS SORCU OYFI TEGU OYODT AHW
LEI NAP SREKA ORCA

Book Talk

"Read me a story!"

"Sorry, Sophie," said Lu. "This book is too scary for you. It'll give you nightmares."

"Ah, come on," whined Sophie. As she lunged for the book, this piece of paper fell out.

26-7-4 27-13-5 26-6-1 27-5-1 26-2-2 26-8-3

"Hey, what's this?"

Clancy snatched it back. "Nothing." He winked at Lu. "Just math homework."

They can't fool me — they're sending secret messages.

How it works

1. The math homework was actually a secret message sent in book code. To use book code, you and your partner both need a copy of the same book. It's important that the same words appear in exactly the same place on both books.

2. To write a word in code, find the word you are looking for in the book. Let's say it is on page 26, line 1, and is the 5th word on that line. The code for this word would be written as 26-1-5.

3. Write the rest of your message using the page number, line and word order. Can you decode the message on Clancy's piece of paper? (Answer on page 40.)

26

took a deep breath as he slipped quietly in the front door of the old mansion. "Oh, maybe I should go home," thought Jack nervously. "I still have to walk the dog and supper will be on the table soon. Why didn't I stay home and eat a bag of cookies?" Suddenly, he heard a creak coming from upstairs somewhere. What was that? His heart started to thump wildly.

He grabbed his lunch bag and blasted out the door. "Dogs breath! I'm outta here! And off he ran as

27

heart was still pounding when he burst through the front door and tripped over the dog. He clicked on their answering machine. The first message was from his mom: "Would you do me a favor and walk the doggy, darling?" No problem — anything to get his mind off how scared he was feeling. He grabbed the dog collar, his baseball cap and a double chocolate chunk cookie, just to tide him over until dinner. "What could I carry for a weapon – just in case whoever was in the old mansion has followed me home!"

27-13-1 27-6-3 26-13-5 27-13-4 27-4-1 26-12-4 26-2-2
26-1-2 27-7-2 26-12-5

Cookie Codes

Clancy put down his chopsticks and licked his lips. "I love Chinese food. What's for dessert?"

Lu passed him a plate of fortune cookies. "Try one of these. They're surprisingly good," she said, with the emphasis on surprise.

When Clancy broke open the cookie, this is what he found:

19-20-21-3-11 2-1-2-25 19-9-20-20-9-14-7 20-8-5 16-5-19-20
20-15-13-15-18-18-15-23 3-1-14 25-15-21 8-5-12-16?

Even Sophie got a coded cookie:

4-1-14-7-5-18 23-9-12-12 3-15-13-5 20-15 20-8-15-19-5
23-8-15 6-15-12-12-15-23 2-9-7 19-9-19-20-5-18

How it works

1. The fortunes in the cookies were written in number code. In this code, you substitute a number for a letter. So A = 1, B = 2, C = 3 and so on. The complete alphabet would look like this:

A	B	C	D	E	F	G	H	I	J	K	L	M	N
1	2	3	4	5	6	7	8	9	10	11	12	13	14

O	P	Q	R	S	T	U	V	W	X	Y	Z
15	16	17	18	19	20	21	22	23	24	25	26

2. A hyphen is put between each letter and a space between words. So the words BONE HEAD would be written 2-15-14-5 8-5-1-4. Can you decode Clancy's and Sophie's fortunes? (Answer on page 40.)

3. To make this code harder to decode, you can shift the numbers one letter. So A = 2, B = 3 and so on. Or shift the code several letters. As long as the person you are sending the message to knows how many letters to shift, she will be able to decode your message.

23-8-1-20 4-15 25-15-21 7-5-20 9-6 25-15-21
3-18-15-19-19 1 16-15-15-4-12-5 23-9-20-8 1 3-8-9-3-11-5-14?
1 16-15-15-3-8-5-4 5-7-7.

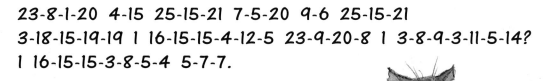

Musical Message

Bright and early the next morning there was a knock at the front door. Lu opened it and found a tuba with a tail. Clancy's head poked out from around the tuba.

"Reporting for baby-sitting duty," he said, saluting. "Hope Sophie's still in bed, because I've got just the right music to wake her up."

How it works

1. Clancy wrote the message in musical code. Each musical note stands for a letter. Can you decode the message Clancy sent to Lu? (Answer on page 40.)

Clancy handed Lu some sheet music and began to play. The "music" sounded like two elephants fighting. Lu looked at the sheet music in her paws. Then she smiled. There was a message for her in the music.

2. To send a message in musical code, first draw five straight horizontal lines to make a musical staff. Join the lines with one vertical line and add a treble clef. Add the musical notes that spell out your message.

3. To write a longer message, you can add lyrics (the words of a song) underneath the music using the reverse code from page 4. The joke below was written this way.

DRATSUM. S'TI EHT TSEB GNIHT ROF A TOH GOD.

Holey Codes

Clancy was poking holes in the newspaper with a pin.

"You're going to get it for wrecking the paper before my mom reads it," growled Sophie.

Clancy peered over the top of the page, smiled at Sophie and passed the paper to Lu.

Sophie tried to grab it — she knew there would be a secret message in it somewhere.

But Lu was too fast for her. She took the paper, held it up to the light and read Clancy's secret message.

This is what Lu saw:

Dognappers hit Barkerville

Two young cocker spaniels were taken from Bark Park yesterday. "Looks like it was a dognapping," police officer Doberman told reporters. A ring of dognappers has been working in neighboring towns over the past few months. Dogs are taken by the thieves and held ransom. They usually demand a large amount of cash.

To protect the citizens of Barkerville from the dognappers, "There are round the clock patrols in all public places." But residents should not let young pups out of their sight until the dognappers are caught." officer Doberman said.

There's nothing but a bunch of holes.

How it works

1. Clancy sent the message in pinprick code. To decode the message, look for the letters that have a pinhole above them. Write down the first pinpricked letter, then the next and so on. Read across and down, as you would read a book. Can you decode the message Clancy sent to Lu? (Answer on page 40.)

2. To send a pinprick message, put a pinprick above the letters in the newspaper that spell out the words of your message. This code works best with short messages. To read the message, hold the newspaper up to the light.

Dognapper

Two young cocker spaniels were taken from Bark Park yesterday. "Looks like it was a dognapping," police officer Doberman told reporters. A ring of dognappers has been rking in neighbori

What do you call a dog that likes to live alone?

Dognappers demand ransom

Dognappers have contacted the worried families of two young dogs who went missing from Bark Park Thursday. "They want money —lots of it," said Mr. C. Spaniel. "They must be stopped."

It was not known if the families would give in to the dognappers' demands.

Crossed Words

Sophie still hadn't figured out Clancy's newspaper message, but Lu understood it perfectly. She quietly flipped to the page of the newspaper with the crossword puzzle. The puzzle was filled in, but not with the correct answers.

Clancy had hidden his message in the crossword. He knew that no one pays attention to a crossword puzzle that's filled in — except an experienced spy.

Crosswords? I'll give them cross words!

How it works

1. Clancy wrote the message in crossword code. To decode it, start reading across from the upper left. All the words are run together, so you'll have to figure out where to break them apart. Can you decode the message Clancy sent to Lu? (Answer on page 40.)

2. To write a crossword code, use any blank crossword puzzle from a newspaper or magazine. Start at the blank box on the upper left and write your message in the blanks. Fill the leftover spaces with any letters you wish.

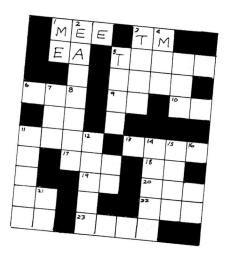

C R O S S W O R D

Steamed!

Tiring Sophie out with a run had been a good idea — until she ran into a huge mud puddle. Now she was singing in the shower, while Lu and Clancy waited for her in the steam-filled bathroom.

A blast of water spurted out of the shower and drenched Lu and Clancy. They had a feeling it was no accident.

How it works

I. Clancy wrote the message in grid code. To decode it, use this grid:

	1	2	3	4	5
1	A	B	C	D	E
2	F	G	H	I	J
3	K	L	M	N	O
4	P	Q	R	S	T
5	U	V	W	X	Y/Z

2. Each letter has a two-digit number. The first digit is the row the letter is found in and the second digit is the column. For example, the letter H is in row 2 and column 3, so it is written as 23.

Clancy looked at the mirror. It was covered with steam. That gave him an idea. As Sophie belted out, "How much is that doggy in the window?" Clancy wrote these numbers on the steamed-up mirror:

11 12-24-22 32-51-34-13-23 44-23-35-51-32-14 41-51-45 23-15-43

45-35 44-32-15-15-41.

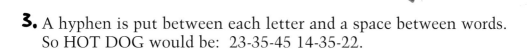

3. A hyphen is put between each letter and a space between words. So HOT DOG would be: 23-35-45 14-35-22.

4. Can you decode the message Clancy wrote on the mirror?
(Answer on page 40.)

53-23-11-45 14-35 14-35-22-44 31-15-15-41 11-45 45-23-15
15-34-45-43-11-34-13-15 45-35 45-23-15-24-43 23-35-51-44-15?

11 53-15-32-13-35-33-15 33-51-45-45.

Noodle Notes

Even after a long run and a shower, Sophie wasn't the least bit worn out. She was still stuck to Lu and Clancy like glue. And now she was splashing tomato sauce all over the kitchen.

"Soooooophie!" yelled Lu. "You're making a mess."

"No, I'm not. I'm making tomato sauce."

Lu rolled her eyes and broke up some dried spaghetti. Her paws moved in a blur and when she was done, this is what Clancy saw:

How it works

1. Lu wrote the message using an ancient alphabet called ogham. She used dry spaghetti, but you can use a pencil and paper. The ogham alphabet uses straight lines to create the letters. It looks like this:

A B C D E F G H I J K L M N O P Q R S T U V W X Y/Z

2. Can you decode the message Lu left for Clancy? (Answer on page 40.)

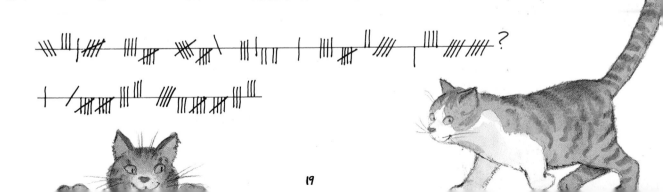

Phony Numbers

Clancy checked the pad of paper by the phone. There was a phone number surrounded by doodles. Or that's what it looked like. But Clancy knew better. It was a coded message.

He was about to decode it, when Sophie stuck her head around the kitchen door. "I'm pooped. I'm going to take a dog nap."

Finally Sophie was going to leave them alone for a while. "Great. Sweet dreams," Clancy said.

He turned back to the coded message.

20

How it works

1. Lu wrote the message in telephone code. It uses the buttons on the phone to represent the letters of the alphabet. It's a great way to hide messages among other numbers on a pad by your telephone or in a phone book.

	ABC	DEF
1	2	3
GHI 4	JKL 5	MNO 6
PRS 7	TUV 8	WXY 9
*	0	#

2. Each number (except 1) has three letters above it. The number 2, for example, has ABC above it. To identify which of the three letters is being used, a special mark is added:

A = 2̀   B = 2̓   C = 2́

3. The whole alphabet in telephone code looks like this:

ABC	DEF	GHI	JKL	MNO	PRS	TUV	WXY	QZ
222	333	444	555	666	777	888	999	10

4. Can you decode the message Lu left for Clancy? (Answer on page 40.)

9428 47 94483 358339 263 22757 ?

7872676.

A Tubular Tale

Lu was snooping around the shed when Clancy bounded in. His tail was wagging so hard it knocked over a rake. "She's asleep! Sophie's finally asleep!" He jumped over a bench.

"Shhhh!" Lu put one paw up to her mouth. She looked around suspiciously and sniffed the air.

"But she's ..." Lu's paw over Clancy's mouth stopped him short.

Motioning him to be quiet, Lu handed Clancy a long strip of paper.

Clancy instantly knew what to do. He grabbed the rake and decoded it.

Lu sent me a scytale, my favorite kind of code.

How it works

1. Lu wrote the message using a coding device called a scytale. To make and use a scytale, cut two paper strips 2.5 cm x 28 cm (1 in. x 11 in.) and tape them end to end, making one long strip.

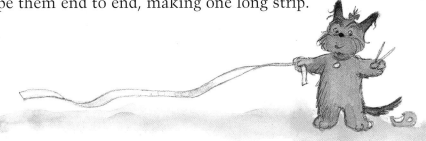

2. Wrap the strip around a cylinder. You can use a rake handle like Clancy did, the cardboard tube from a roll of paper towel, or a rolling pin — any cylinder will work. Overlap the edges of the paper slightly. Tape the ends in place.

3. Write your message across the paper as shown. Use more than one line if you wish. Carefully unwrap the paper and give it to your spy partner.

4. To decode the message, your partner wraps the strip around an identical or same-sized cylinder.

Message in a Map

Where was Sophie? The two baby-sitters looked everywhere for her. She wasn't in her room sleeping or messing up the kitchen. She wasn't watching TV. And she definitely wasn't stuck to them like glue.

"Maybe she's in the tree house," Clancy suggested.

How it works

1. The message was written in tree code. Use the grid on page 16 to create a "tree" alphabet. Each number from the grid is drawn as one branch on a tree. For example, the letter H is in row 2, column 3.
To draw the letter H in the tree alphabet, first draw a trunk: | .
Next, draw two branches on the left side of the tree ⅄
and three branches on the right side of the trunk ⑂ .

So, the word BONE is written ⑂ ⑂ ⑂ ⑂ .
Can you decode the message found by Lu and Clancy? (Answer on page 40.)

2. When writing in tree code, leave a space between the words so that the trees are clumped together.

But when they climbed up to take a look, there was no sign of Sophie, just a map nailed to the wall.

"What's the map of, Lu?"

Lu peered at it closely. "I don't think it's a map. I think it's a code. But if you didn't make it —" Clancy shook his head "— and I didn't make it, who did?"

"Whoever did knows our secret tree code."

Sophie's been dognapped!

3. Add lakes, mountains, roads, houses and other landmarks to make it look more like a map. You can even make your "map" look old and yellowed by brushing it with tea and crumpling it slightly.

Tic Tac Toe Code

Lu and Clancy were in shock. Someone else knew their codes. And Sophie was missing. Just then a paper airplane sailed in through a window and landed on the floor of the tree house.

Lu picked it up. She was about to send it flying back out when some squiggles on the side of the plane caught her eye. She peered closely at them.

Here is what Lu saw:

⊐⊔<<⊔> <⊔⊓◻ ⊐⊔⊏□ ⊐⊐⊐
⊏⊔⊏⊓⊓◻ ⊏ ⊏⊏□⊐⊓ ⊓⊔ ⊓⊓◻
⊐□∨⊓ ⊏<⊓□

How it works

1. The message was sent in tic tac toe code. Here is the letter key for tic tac toe code:

A	B	C
D	E	F
G	H	I

N	O	P
Q	R	S
T	U	V

2. The tic tac toe alphabet is taken from the letter key and looks like this:

⊐ ⊔ ⊏ ⊐ □ ⊏ ⊓ ⊓ ⊏ > ∨ < ∧ ⊐ ⊔ ⊏ ⊐ □ ⊏
A B C D E F G H I J K L M N O P Q R S

⊓ ⊓ ⊏ > ∨ < ∧
T U V W X Y Z

3. Can you decode the tic tac toe message that was sent to Lu and Clancy?
(Answer on page 40.)

⊐⊓⊐⊓ ⊐⊔ <⊔◻ ⊓⊐⊓ ⊏⊏ <⊔◻ ⊏□⊔⊏⊏
⊐ ⊏⊔⊏∨□□⊏⊏⊐⊐⊓□< ⊐ □⊔⊔⊏⊓□□
⊐⊐⊐ ⊐ ⊏⊔⊔⊐<□?
⊏⊔⊏∨-⊐-⊏⊔⊔⊐<□-⊐⊔⊔◻

Wheelin' Words

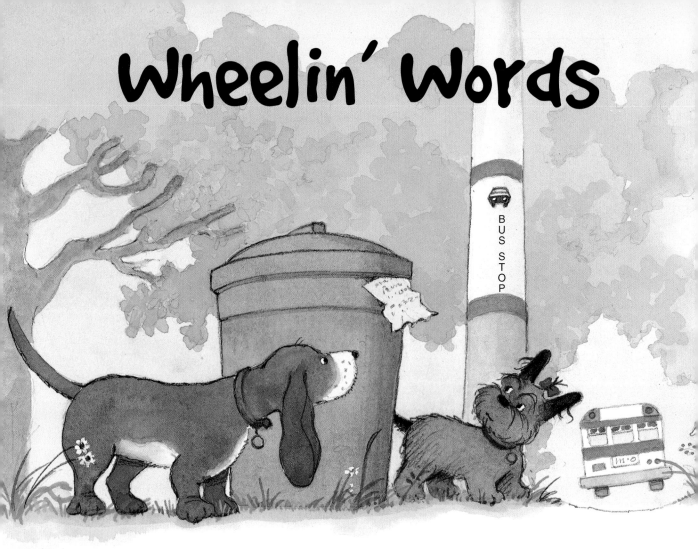

Lu and Clancy (who were super sniffers, as well as super sleuths) followed Sophie's scent to the bus stop down the street.

"Oh-no ... her scent has disappeared. The dognappers must have taken her on the bus," cried Lu.

But Clancy's nose was still sniffing. It led him to a note hanging out of a garbage can. When he tried to pull it out, a wheel made out of two paper plates came with it. This note was attached to the plates:

♡⇕⇕▲ ⌂✳ ⊫⊨|ℂ≈ 8⌂✳⊡⇕8 ⇕∅

⇕⊡♡≈⊢ ⇕∅ 🐱⇕⇕⊡♡≈⊢

"It's a code wheel!" exclaimed Lu. "Quick, use it to decode the message! Maybe it will lead us to Sophie."

How it works

1. A code wheel is actually two wheels. The smaller, inner one has the letters of the alphabet around it. The larger, outer one has symbols such as # and %. To use the code wheel, you have to know which symbol to line up with the letter A. To decode the dognappers's message, line up # with the letter A.

(Answer on page 40.)

2. To make your own code wheel, print the alphabet around the edge of a small paper plate. Space the letters as equally as possible.

3. Put the small plate on top of a larger paper plate. Use a large paper clip to hold the two plates together. On the large plate, draw one symbol opposite each letter.

4. Use a pencil to punch a hole through the center of each plate. Fasten them together with a paper fastener. Remove the paper clip.

5. Line up the letter A with any symbol you wish. Then write your message using the symbols opposite the letters. To decode your message, all your partner needs to know is which letter you lined up with the letter A.

Reflective Secrets

oodles of poodles

MISSING

CUTE BROWN PUPPY
ANSWERING TO THE NAME of SOPHIE
PUZZLED? SANDBOX
HOLDS NEXT CLUE

"Has Sophie been sold to the pet store? Oh no! Maybe we're too late, Clancy!"

Lu and Clancy stared into the window of Oodles of Poodles. There were some cute kittens — if you liked cats. And there was a very mean-looking parrot. But there was no brown pup.

The two friends were about to go into the pet store and demand the owner hand over Sophie when ...

"Look," cried Clancy. He noticed a poster in a corner of the store window.

How it works

1. The dognappers wrote this message using backwards code. To decode it, hold a mirror up to the message and look into the mirror.
(Answer on page 40.)

2. In backwards code, the letters of the alphabet look like this:

A B C D E F G H I J K L M N O P Q R S T U V W X Y Z

3. Use the backwards alphabet to write your message. Start in the upper right corner of the paper. Some people say you can trick yourself into writing backwards by putting an index card on your forehead and writing on it from left to right. Try it with a short word like HELP.

Don't think too hard about it as you're doing it. The writing comes out backwards because the right and left sides of your brain get confused when you write this way.

We Zig, They Zag

"I found it," cried Clancy, holding up a large envelope.

"What does it say?"

Clancy began to read, "Asmltip ..." He stopped and untied his tongue. "Must be some foreign language."

Lu shook her head. "Looks like zigzag code to me."

How it works

1. Zigzag code is written up and down on two lines. Write the first letter of the message on a piece of paper. Directly below the first letter, write the second letter in the word. The next letter in the word goes on the first line and so on.

SOPHIE =
S P I
O H E

2. There are no spaces between the words. So the phrase FIRE HYDRANT would be written like this:

F R H D A T
I E Y R N

Can you decode the message Lu and Clancy found? (Answer on page 40.)

WAI PRLWTLNLG
HTSUPEIHOGES

ARPDN
GAEAE

The Puzzler

Lu and Clancy shook the envelope they had found in the sandbox. A flurry of puzzle pieces fell out. Each piece had letters on the back.

"Must be the next clue," said Clancy, starting to assemble the puzzle.

Lu looked at her watch and panicked. "Mom will be home in half an hour. If I don't find Sophie by then, I'm going to be in the dog house."

How it works

1. You can make your own jigsaw puzzle code. Cut off the front of an empty cereal box. Draw some crisscrossing wavy lines on the back of it. The more lines you draw, the more difficult your puzzle will be.

2. Write your message on the cardboard. It doesn't matter if the words go across lines or in the spaces between the lines.

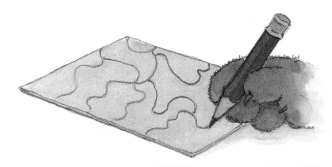

Clancy was working as fast as he could. He put in the last few pieces and saw that he had assembled a picture of Sophie. It was so sloppy it looked like something Sophie herself might have drawn. Clancy carefully turned over the puzzle and this message appeared on the back.

DELIVER A CHOCOLATE CAKE WITH LIVER ICING TO THE TREE HOUSE AND GET SOPHIE BACK.

—THE DOGNAPPERS

Chocolate cake with liver icing? Hmmm ... that's one of Sophie's favorites.

3. Cut along the lines. Your spy partner will have to assemble the puzzle to read the message.

What do dogs wear when they bicycle?

A Sweet Code

"Yoo-hoo, dognappers," Clancy called. "Here's your cake. Now where's our Sophie?"

There was no answer. Out of the corner of her eye, Lu saw her mom's car coming down the road. "Pleeease, dognappers. I'd do anything to get her back."

A voice that sounded muffled but familiar wafted out of the tree house.

"Will you play with Sophie and be nice to her?"

"Anything."

"Okay, bring up the cake but don't try any funny stuff."

Lu and Clancy carried the cake up the ladder and into the tree house. From behind the bookshelf they heard a snicker, and Sophie poked out her head.

"Hot diggity dog! I sure sent you two on a wild-puppy chase!"

"Aw, we figured it out ages ago," said Lu. But a look of relief swept over her face.

Clancy slid the cake toward Sophie. "Now it's your turn. There's a secret message on the cake. Can you figure it out?"

How it works

1. Lu and Clancy decorated the cake using Morse code. Morse code is made up of dots • and dashes —. This is what Morse code looks like.

A • —	H • • • •	O — — —	V • • • —
B — • • •	I • •	P • — — •	W • — —
C — • — •	J • — — —	Q — — • —	X — • • —
D — • •	K — • —	R • — •	Y — • — —
E •	L • — • •	S • • •	Z — — • •
F • • — •	M — —	T —	
G — — •	N — •	U • • —	

Can you decode the message sent to Lu and Clancy? (Answer on page 40.)

2. You can also send Morse code by flashlight. A short flash of light is a dot; a longer one is a dash. Or you can send it with a pen on a table. Put the cap on the pen and tap it on the table for a dot; scratch it on the table for a dash.

• — — • • • • • — • •   — • • — — —   — • • — — — — — • • • •

• — — • • —   • — • — • —   — • • • • • • • • — • •

— • — • • — • — • • • ?

• • — •   — • • • • — • — • — • • • — • — — •   • — • • — — — — • • •

Seeing Red

Sophie was dog tired after her exciting day. She headed for bed and was just about to curl up when she spotted a sheet of paper on her pillow with red scribbles all over it. She peered at it. Was it a secret message? Lu and Clancy appeared at her door. Lu handed her a pair of paper glasses with red cellophane lenses. "Here. Try these."

Sophie put on the glasses and looked at the paper. This is what she saw:

This is to certify that Sophie Chandler has been admitted as a spy-in-training in Two Dogs Inc.

signed
Lu & Clancy

Sophie let out a big howl. "Yippee, yahooooo!" She gave Lu and Clancy each a sloppy, wet lick and crawled into bed very tired — and very happy.

How it works

1. Lu and Clancy sent their message in red code. First, they wrote their message faintly in blue pencil crayon.

2. Then they lightly scribbled over the message in red pencil crayon.

3. To make the message appear, it had to be viewed through red cellophane, such as the kind you wrap presents in.

Answers

Pages 4-5
Message: Sophie is on our trail. Meet in tree house at four.
Joke: What do you get if you cross a frog and a dog?
A croaker spaniel.

Pages 6-7
Message: Stay for supper. Message in cookies.
Joke: What do dogs carry their lunch in?
A doggy bag.

Pages 8-9
Clancy's message: Stuck baby-sitting the pest tomorrow. Can you help?
Sophie's message: Danger will come to those who follow big sister.
Joke: What do you get if you cross a poodle with a chicken?
A pooched egg.

Pages 10-11
Message: No talking today. Codes only.
Joke: What should you give a dog with a fever?
Mustard. It's the best thing for a hot dog.

Pages 12-13
Message: Crossword.
Joke: What do you call a dog that likes to live alone?
A hermutt.

Pages 14-15
Message: Let's take a long run to put Sophie to sleep.
Joke: What do dogs like to drive?
Muttacycles.

Pages 16-17
Message: A big lunch should put her to sleep.
Joke: What do dogs keep at the entrance to their house?
A welcome mutt.

Pages 18-19
Message: Message coming by phone.
Joke: What do you call a dog's kiss?
A pooch smooch.

Pages 20-21
Message: Meet in shed.
Joke: What is white, fluffy and barks?
Pupcorn.

Pages 24-25
Message: We have Sophie. Leave the police dogs out of this or else.
Joke: What did Lu and Clancy say when Sophie was dognapped?
Dog-gone.

Pages 26-27
Message: Follow your nose and Sophie's scent to the next clue.
Joke: What do you get if you cross a cocker spaniel, a rooster and a poodle?
Cock-a-poodle-doo.

Pages 28-29
Message: Look in the window of Oodles of Poodles.

Pages 30-31
Message: Puzzled? Sandbox holds next clue.
Joke: Knock, knock.
Who's there?
Olive.
Olive who?
Olive secret messages.

Pages 32-33
Message: Assemble this puzzle
Quick hurry up
And you will discover
Who dognapped the pup
Joke: What is purple with long legs?
A grape dane.

Pages 34-35
Joke: What do dogs wear when they bicycle?
Helmutts.

Pages 36-37
Message: You are in for a surprise.
Joke: Where do dogs park their cars?
In barking lots.